Playful Pet Projects

Get Crafting for Your

DELIGHTFUL DOG

by Ruth Owen

BEARPORT
PUBLISHING

Minneapolis, Minnesota

CREATE!

Library of Congress Cataloging-in-Publication Data

Names: Owen, Ruth, 1967- author.
Title: Get crafting for your delightful dog / Ruth Owen.
Description: Create! books edition. | Minneapolis, Minnesota : Bearport Publishing Company, [2021] | Series: Playful pet projects | Includes bibliographical references and index.
Identifiers: LCCN 2020042148 (print) | LCCN 2020042149 (ebook) | ISBN 9781647476618 (library binding) | ISBN 9781647476687 (ebook)
Subjects: LCSH: Dogs–Equipment and supplies–Juvenile literature. | Handicraft–Juvenile literature.
Classification: LCC SF427.15 .O94 2021 (print) | LCC SF427.15 (ebook) | DDC 636.7–dc23
LC record available at https://lccn.loc.gov/2020042148
LC ebook record available at https://lccn.loc.gov/2020042149

For more information, write to Bearport Publishing, 5357 Penn Avenue South, Minneapolis, MN 55419. Printed in the United States of America.

CONTENTS

GET CRAFTY WITH YOUR DOG

If you love spending time with your dog and enjoy crafting, this is the book for you! Discover four cool craft projects that are fun to make and will give you and your best **canine** pal hours of enjoyment.

◀ **Home Sweet Home**
Does your pet sleep in a boring bed? Your delightful dog deserves a **unique**, handmade shark bed where it can chill out!

Pet Snacks and Treats ▶
Do you like gingerbread? Your dog might, too! Bake a batch of these special, dog-friendly cookies.

◀ **Time to Play**
Dogs can keep their brains and bodies active with toys. Keep your smart pooch happy with this terrific tug tarantula!

◀ Dress It Up

Are you over the moon about your pup? Dress your doggy in this awesome jet pack costume. Your pal will be an adorable space pup!

Have Fun and Be Safe

Crafting for your delightful dog can be lots of fun. But it's important that both you and your pet stay safe by following these top tips for careful crafting.

- Always get permission from an adult before making the projects in this book.

- Read the instructions carefully, and ask an adult for help if there's something you don't understand.

- Be careful when using scissors, and never let your dog touch or play with them.

- Keep any glue or paint where your pet can't sniff, lick, or touch it.

- When your project is complete, recycle any extra paper, cardboard, or packaging. If you have leftover materials, keep them for a future project.

- Clean up when you've finished working.

- Remember! Many dogs do well with lots of touching, play, and attention. But others do better with less.

Never force your dog to do something it seems unhappy to do.

SUPER TOOTHY SHARK BED

Every dog needs a cozy place where it can feel safe. With a cardboard box and lots of creativity, you can make your dog its very own toothy shark bed!

This bed will fit a small to medium-sized dog. You can make the bed larger by using a bigger box.

You will need

- A corrugated cardboard box that's about 20 inches (51 cm) long, 16 in (40.6 cm) wide, and 16 in (40.6 cm) tall
- An adult helper
- Scissors
- Wide tape that can be painted
- A ruler
- A black marker
- A dinner plate
- Tacky glue
- Paint and paintbrushes

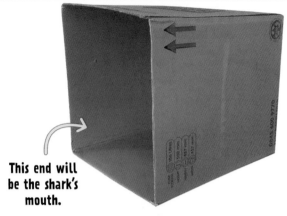

This end will be the shark's mouth.

1 Ask your adult helper to cut off one of the smaller ends of the box. Set aside the scraps to use later. This open end will be the shark's mouth.

2 Tape the remaining sides of the box closed.

3 To make the shark's toothy grin, measure halfway down one side of the mouth opening and make a mark. Then, use a ruler and marker to draw a 10 in (25 cm) horizontal line from the mark across the long side of the box. Repeat on the other side.

4 Next, draw lines from the top and bottom corners of the mouth side of the box to the end of the line you've just drawn. Do this on both sides.

5 Using the marker, draw triangular teeth on the lines you made in step 4.

6 Ask your adult helper to cut out the mouth, leaving the teeth.

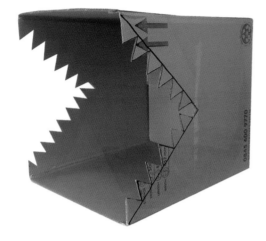

7 To make the shark's top **dorsal fin**, lay the dinner plate on one of the scrap pieces of cardboard. Trace around the top left-hand quarter of the plate, as shown.

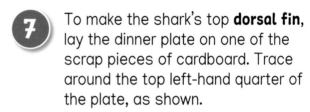

Trace here

8 Next, move the plate to the right so the edge of the plate meets the end of your line at about the 10:00 spot on a clock. Trace around the left edge of the plate to make the other side of the fin. Finally, connect the bottom of the two curved sides with a straight line. Ask your adult helper to cut out the fin.

9 To make the shark's **pectoral fins** draw two triangles on some scrap cardboard. The three sides of each triangle should be about 6 in (15 cm) long. Ask your helper to cut them out.

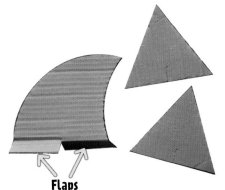

Flaps

10 Now, ask your helper to cut a 1 in (2.5 cm) slot into the bottom center of each fin. Then, folding up from the bottom, bend one side of the bottom edge backward and the other side forward. These folded parts are flaps that can be glued to the box.

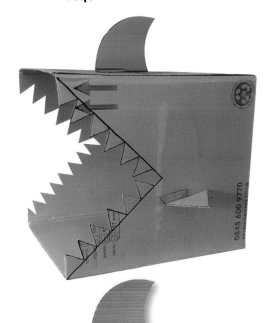

11 Add glue to the bottom of the flaps on the fins. Stick the dorsal fin to the top of the box. Then, glue one pectoral fin to each side just behind the mouth.

12 When the glue has dried, paint your shark.

13 Once the paint is completely dry, put a blanket inside the shark and introduce your pup to its *jaw*-some new bed!

SWEET SHARK DREAMS!

DELICIOUS DOGGY GINGERBREAD

Always feed your dog healthy food that contains all the **nutrients** it needs. As an occasional treat, make your dog these spicy, doggy-shaped cookies. This **recipe** will make nine treats.

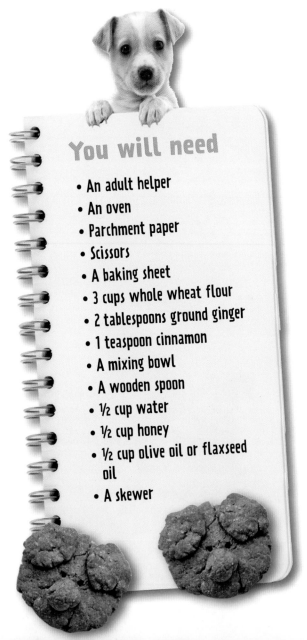

You will need

- An adult helper
- An oven
- Parchment paper
- Scissors
- A baking sheet
- 3 cups whole wheat flour
- 2 tablespoons ground ginger
- 1 teaspoon cinnamon
- A mixing bowl
- A wooden spoon
- ½ cup water
- ½ cup honey
- ½ cup olive oil or flaxseed oil
- A skewer

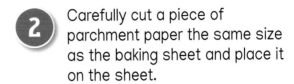

1 Ask an adult helper to preheat the oven to 325°F (160°C).

2 Carefully cut a piece of parchment paper the same size as the baking sheet and place it on the sheet.

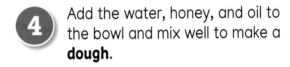

3 Put the flour, ginger, and cinnamon into the mixing bowl. Stir with a wooden spoon until the **ingredients** are combined.

4 Add the water, honey, and oil to the bowl and mix well to make a **dough**.

Mix well

Gingerbread dough

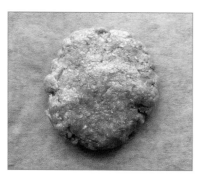

5 Using your hands, roll a piece of dough into a ball about the size of a golf ball. Then, press it into a circle about ½ in (1.25 cm) thick. Place the circle on the baking sheet.

6 Now, add the dog's ears. Using your hands, roll some dough into a ball about the size of a grape. Shape it into an oval about ¼ in (0.6 cm) thick. Press it into the top left of the circle you made in step 5. Repeat to make a second ear, pressing it into the top right.

7 Next, roll a pea-sized dough ball and press it into the center of the face for a nose.

8 Finally, use a skewer to make two holes above the nose for the eyes.

9 Repeat steps 5 through 8 to make more cookies until all the dough is used up.

Baked cookies

10 Ask your adult helper to put the gingerbread treats into the oven and bake them for 20 minutes.

11 After the cookies are baked, allow them to cool completely. Then, your dog can enjoy a spicy, crunchy treat!

SNIFF . . . SNIFF . . . DO I SMELL DOGGY GINGERBREAD?

These cookies should only be fed to your dog as a rare treat. Eating too many will make your pet unhealthy.

TARANTULA TUG TOY

Have you ever seen your dog crouch down on its front legs with its bottom in the air? This body language says: Let's play. Get cutting and braiding to make your playful pal this terrific tug toy with eight legs!

You will need

- 2 old, adult-sized T-shirts in different colors
- Scissors
- A tape measure
- A tennis ball

1 Take one T-shirt and carefully cut through both layers of fabric just below the sleeves.

2 Next, cut up one side of the shirt to make a single long piece of fabric.

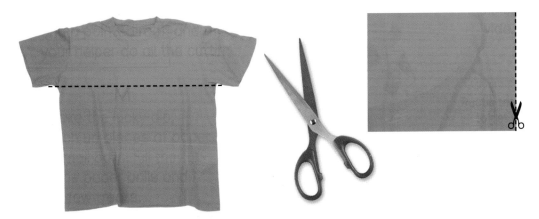

3 Lay the fabric flat. Measure and cut two strips that are 10 in (25 cm) wide.

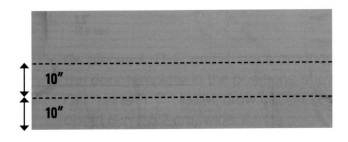

10"

10"

4 Repeat steps 1 through 3 with the second T-shirt.

5 Cut a strip of fabric that's about 1 in (2.5 cm) wide and 12 in (30.5 cm) long to use as a tying strip.

6 Lay one strip of fabric flat. Then, lay a second strip in the same color on top, making an X shape. Add the third and fourth strips, making a star shape with alternating colors, as shown.

7 Place the tennis ball in the center of the fabric star.

8 Then, take one end of the top strip of fabric and bring its two short ends together so the tennis ball is wrapped inside.

The tennis ball is in here.

9 Repeat with the other three strips.

The ball is in here.

10 Take the tying strip and tie it tightly around the bunch of strips just below the tennis ball.

11 Carefully cut one strip of fabric into three equal long strips. Be careful not to cut off any fabric.

12 Tightly braid the three narrow strips you just cut. Stop braiding about 3 in (7.5 cm) from the bottom. Tie the three ends in two or three tight double knots to keep the braid from unraveling. You've just made one leg.

End of the braid

13 Repeat steps 11 and 12 with the remaining seven strips of fabric.

14 When all the strips are braided, your tarantula tug toy will be ready for your delightful dog.

LET THE TUG FUN BEGIN!

SPACE PUP JET PACK

Everyone has heard of astronauts. But how about turning your pet into a daring astro-dog with its own pup jet pack made of items from your family's recycling?

You will need

- An adult helper
- A measuring tape
- A pen and paper
- 2 large sheets of poster board
- A pencil
- A ruler
- Scissors
- A roll of heavy-duty aluminum foil
- Tacky glue
- Silver duct tape
- 2 pieces of Velcro that are 1 in (2.5 cm) long
- 2 large, empty plastic soda bottles
- Silver paint
- A paintbrush
- 1 sheet of red craft foam
- 1 sheet of yellow craft foam
- Tacky glue

If you're making a jet pack for a small dog, you can use smaller plastic bottles.

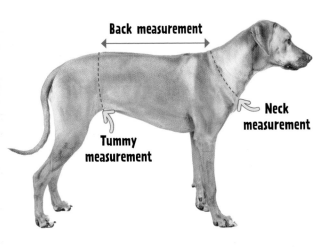

Back measurement

Neck measurement

Tummy measurement

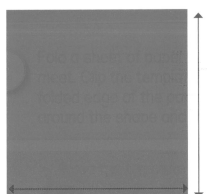

Length of the back

Width of the back plus 4 extra inches

2 extra inches for fastening

2 extra inches for fastening

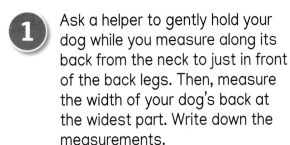

1 Ask a helper to gently hold your dog while you measure along its back from the neck to just in front of the back legs. Then, measure the width of your dog's back at the widest part. Write down the measurements.

2 Next, carefully measure around the lower part of your dog's neck. Measure around its tummy, just in front of its back legs. Write down the measurements.

3 To make the jacket part of the jet pack, draw a rectangle on the poster board using your dog's back measurements. Add an extra 4 in (10 cm) to the width of the jacket, so it will wrap around your dog's sides. Cut out the jacket.

4 To make the jacket's fastening strips, measure and draw a strip of cardboard 1 in (2.5 cm) wide and your dog's neck measurement plus an extra 2 in (5 cm) long. Cut out the strip.

5 Then, measure and draw a second strip that is 2 in (5 cm) wide and the tummy measurement plus an extra 2 in (5 cm) long. Cut out this piece, too.

6 Lay out a piece of aluminum foil that is twice as wide as the jacket paper. Cover one side of the cardboard jacket with glue, and stick it to the center of the foil.

> Depending on the size of your roll of foil, you may need to use two or more pieces.

7 Wrap the jacket shape in the foil as you might wrap a gift. Fasten the foil with duct tape. This will be the underside of the jacket.

8 Wrap the two fastening strips in the same way you have wrapped the jacket piece.

9 Take one portion of Velcro. Stick the two halves to opposite ends of the neck strip, making sure that the clean, outside part of the strip forms a loop when the Velcro is stuck together. Repeat with the tummy strip.

10 Glue the fastening strips tape side up onto the underside of the jacket at each short end. Then, tape the fastening strips to the jacket for extra strength.

Outside part of strip

Outside part of strip

Velcro

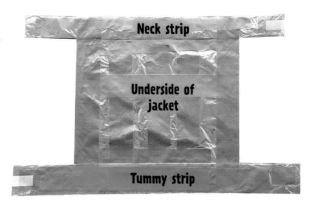

Neck strip

Underside of jacket

Tummy strip

11 To make the jet pack, remove the caps and labels from the two bottles and paint them silver. Add a second coat of paint if needed. Allow them to dry.

12 Now, draw flame shapes on the foam sheets, making sure that the base of each flame will fit snugly into the neck of the bottles. Cut out the flames.

13 Take half the foam flames and push their narrow ends into one bottle. Then, wrap the neck of the bottle with duct tape to hold the flames in place. Repeat with the other bottle.

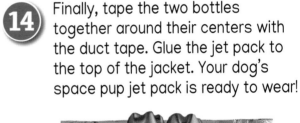

14 Finally, tape the two bottles together around their centers with the duct tape. Glue the jet pack to the top of the jacket. Your dog's space pup jet pack is ready to wear!

5, 4, 3, 2, 1 . . .
BLASTOFF!

TOP TIPS FOR A HEALTHY, HAPPY DOG!

Being a **responsible** dog owner is all about keeping your pet healthy. Here are 10 tips to help you take care of your precious pup pal.

1 If your dog eats too much, it can become overweight and unhealthy. Ask your vet how much your dog should eat.

Overweight   **Healthy weight**

2 Never feed your dog chocolate, onions, grapes, raisins, or currants. If your dog eats these things, contact your vet immediately!

3 Make sure your dog always has plenty of fresh water to drink, and wash its water bowl daily.

4 Give your dog plenty of exercise to keep it active and healthy.

5 Dog poop can cause other animals and people to get sick. Always pick up your dog's poop and throw it away.

6 Never leave a dog alone in a car. The temperature can quickly rise or drop and become dangerous.

7 When the weather is hot, walk your dog in the early morning and in the evening. This will keep your dog from overheating.

8 Your dog might feel anxious when it's left home alone. Leaving a radio on with the volume down low can be comforting to a dog that's on its own.

9 Train your dog from an early age using **rewards**. Never shout at your dog. This can make your dog nervous and afraid of you.

10 A dog may live for 12 years or longer. Be sure you are willing to care for your pet for all this time!

GLOSSARY

canine a dog or other member of the dog family

dorsal fin a single fin on the back of a shark, fish, dolphin, or whale

dough a thick, sticky mixture of flour, water, and other ingredients that is used to make cookies, cakes, and breads

ingredients the substances that are used to make food

nutrients things that are found in food that keep people and animals healthy

pectoral fins flap-like parts located on the sides of a fish that help it to move through the water

recipe a set of instructions for making a particular dish or type of food

responsible caring, trustworthy, and in charge

rewards things given to an animal or person for hard work, getting something right, or another achievement

unique one of a kind

INDEX

READ MORE

Colson, Mary. *The Truth About Dogs: What Dogs Do When You're Not Looking (Pets Uncovered!).* Chicago: Heinemann–Raintree, 2017.

Vink, Amanda. *Is a Dog a Good Pet for Me? (The Best Pet for Me).* New York: PowerKids Press, 2020.

LEARN MORE ONLINE

1. Go to **www.factsurfer.com**
2. Enter "**Crafting Dog**" into the search box.
3. Click on the cover of this book to see a list of websites.

ABOUT THE AUTHOR

Ruth Owen has been developing and writing children's books for more than 10 years. She lives in Cornwall, England, just minutes from the ocean. Ruth's best canine pals, Bobby and Sybil, live next door and she loves taking them for walks. Bobby even helped out with this book by modeling the space pup jet pack on page 18!